SPECTRUM®

Manuscript Handwriting

Grades K–2

Published by Spectrum®
an imprint of Carson-Dellosa Publishing
Greensboro, NC

Spectrum®
An imprint of Carson-Dellosa Publishing LLC
P.O. Box 35665
Greensboro, NC 27425 USA

ISBN 978-1-4838-1380-6

02-080177811

Table of Contents

Manuscript

About This Book

This *Spectrum® Manuscript Handwriting* workbook provides the support your child needs to master handwriting in manuscript (printed) form. Lessons demonstrate proper formation of both uppercase and lowercase letters and provide practice in writing letters, words, and sentences.

Because lowercase letters are generally more challenging to form, practice pages are ordered based on the hand movements used to write in lowercase. They begin with counter-clockwise curves and progress through down strokes, diagonal strokes, and down strokes with clockwise curves.

a d g q c e o u s f	counter-clockwise curves
l i t j	down strokes
k y v w x z	diagonal strokes
m n r h b p	down strokes with clockwise curves

Chapter I introduces each uppercase and lowercase letter, providing guiding arrows for proper letter formation.

Students are then asked to trace and write words that make use of that letter. To provide exposure to content-area vocabulary, these words are pulled from vocabulary lists for students in kindergarten through grade 2.

In **Chapter 2**, students copy silly sentences and tongue twisters inspired by words in Chapter I, and in the **Final Review**, they write sentences containing all 26 letters of the alphabet. These fun, creative exercises might just inspire students to put their handwriting skills to work in stories or silly sentences of their own.

Aa Bb Cc Dd

Ee Ff Gg Hh

Ii Jj Kk Ll

Mm Nn Oo Pp

Qq Rr Ss Tt

Uu Vv Ww Xx

Yy Zz

418 Cloverly Forest Dr.
Silver Spring, MD 20905

Write your full name. Jadon Edem Baumblatt

Jadon Edem Baumblatt

418 Cloverly Forest Dr.

Spring, MD 20905

Write your age. Spell out the number. 6 Six

6 Six

Write today's date. Use a word for the month. 3/15/2018

March 15, 2018

March 15, 2018

312-804-8939
312-804-8938
3128048938
3128048938

4 4

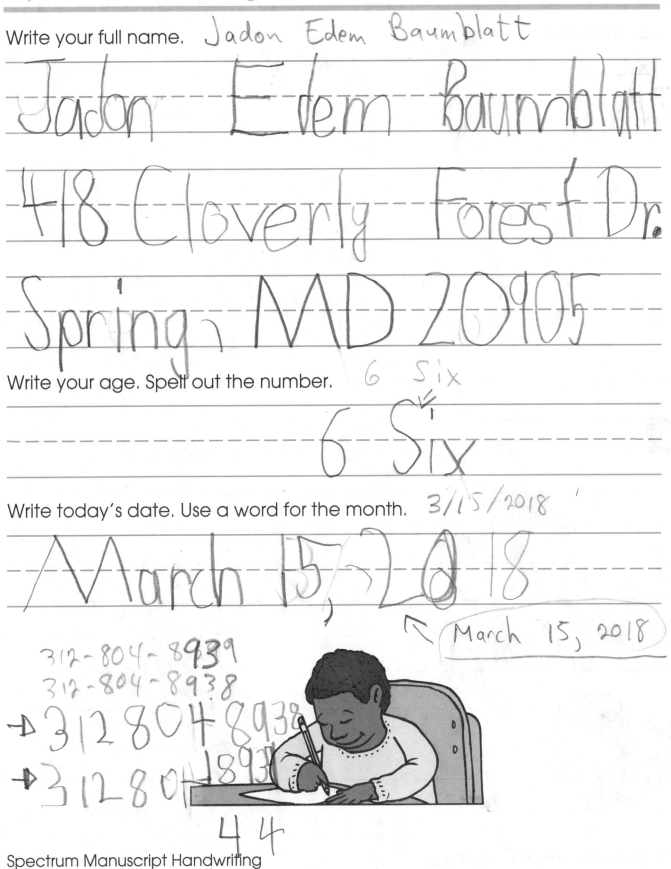

Trace and write.

Spectrum Manuscript Handwriting
Grades K–2

8

Chapter 1 Lesson 1
Letters and Words

Lesson 1.1   The Letter **Aa**

Trace and write.

Alaska

alphabet

air

add

Lesson 1.2   The Letter **Dd**

Trace and write.

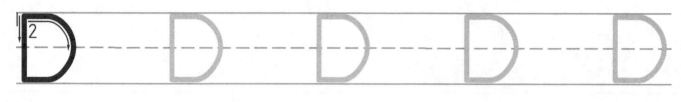

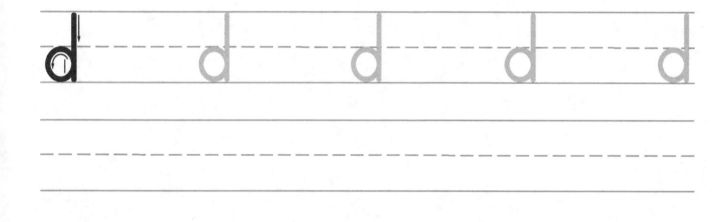

Lesson 1.2 The Letter **Dd**

Trace and write.

Delaware

draft

data

day

Lesson 1.3   The Letter **Gg**

Trace and write.

G   G   G   G   G

g   g   g   g   g

Lesson 1.3   The Letter **Gg**

Trace and write.

Georgia

grammar

gather

grow

Lesson 1.4   The Letter **Qq**

Trace and write.

Lesson 1.4 The Letter **Qq**

Trace and write.

Quebec

question

quarter

queen

Lesson 1.5 The Letter **Cc**

Trace and write.

C   C   C   C   C

c   c   c   c   c

Spectrum Manuscript Handwriting
Grades K–2

Chapter 1 Lesson 5
Letters and Words

Lesson 1.5   The Letter **Cc**

Trace and write.

California

circle

cloud

cave

Lesson 1.6   The Letter **Ee**

Trace and write.

E   E   E   E   E

e   e   e   e   e

ENERGY

Lesson 1.6 The Letter **Ee**

Trace and write.

English

energy

eight

edit

Lesson 1.7 The Letter Oo

Trace and write.

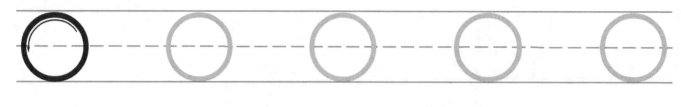

Lesson 1.7   The Letter **Oo**

Trace and write.

Oklahoma

organize

octopus

oval

Lesson 1.8   The Letter **Uu**

Trace and write.

Lesson 1.8 The Letter **Uu**

Trace and write.

United States

unique

uncle

unit

Lesson 1.9   The Letter **Ss**

Trace and write.

S S S S S

s s s s s

Lesson 1.9 The Letter **Ss**

Trace and write.

Seattle

statement

square

stars

Lesson 1.10 The Letter **Ff**

Trace and write.

Lesson 1.10 The Letter **Ff**

Trace and write.

Florida - - - - - - - - - - -

fraction - - - - - - - - -

force - - - - - - - - - - -

fifth - - - - - - - - - - - -

Lesson 1.11 The Letter **Ll**

Trace and write.

Lesson 1.11 The Letter **Ll**

Trace and write.

Lincoln

letter

length

land

Lesson 1.12 The Letter **Ii**

Trace and write.

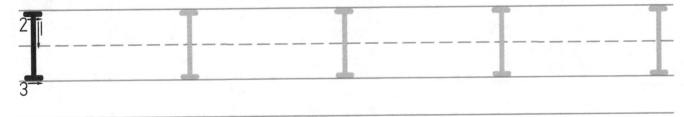

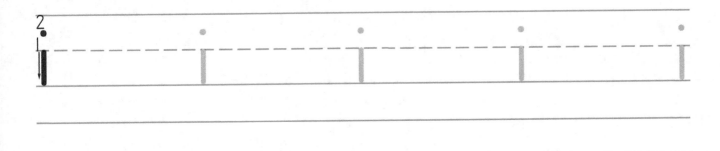

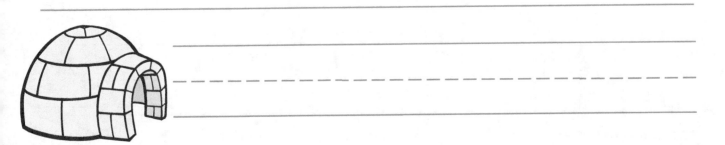

Lesson 1.12 The Letter **Ii**

Trace and write.

Indiana

inform

igloo

inch

Lesson 1.13 The Letter **Tt**

Trace and write.

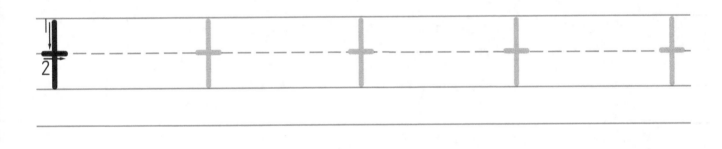

Lesson 1.13 The Letter **Tt**

Trace and write.

Texas

temperature

tenth

title

Lesson 1.14   The Letter **Jj**

Trace and write.

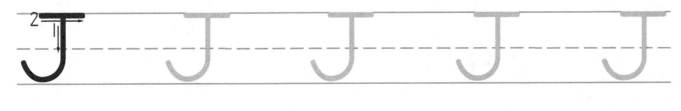

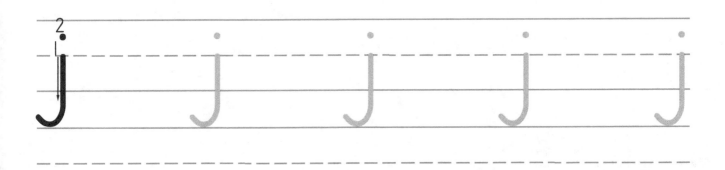

Lesson 1.14 The Letter **Jj**

Trace and write.

Jefferson

July

jaguar

judge

Lesson 1.15 The Letter **Kk**

Trace and write.

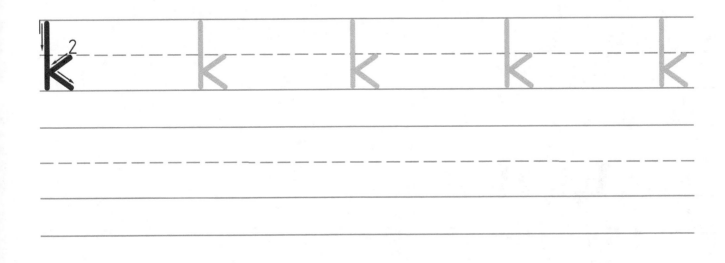

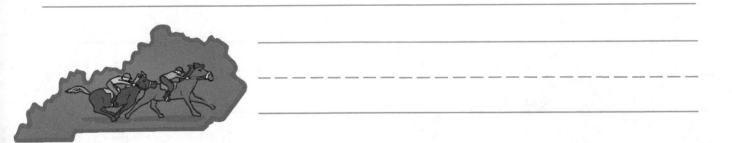

Lesson 1.15 The Letter **Kk**

Trace and write.

Kentucky

Kennedy

kilometer

key

Lesson 1.16   The Letter **Yy**

Trace and write.

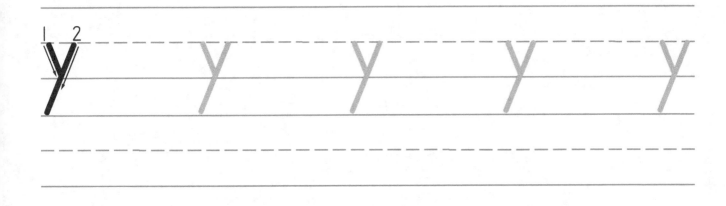

Lesson 1.16 The Letter **Yy**

Trace and write.

Yukon

York

yogurt

yak

Lesson 1.17   The Letter **Vv**

Trace and write.

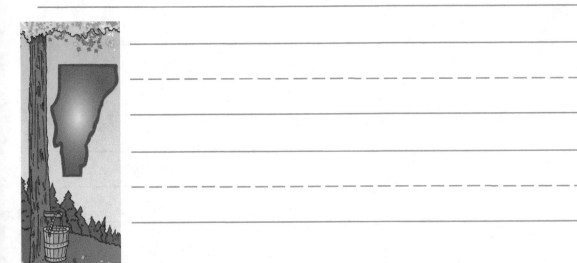

Lesson 1.17 The Letter **Vv**

Trace and write.

Vermont

volume

vowel

verb

Lesson 1.18 The Letter **Ww**

Trace and write.

Lesson 1.18   The Letter **Ww**

Trace and write.

Washington

weight

water

wind

Lesson 1.19 The Letter **Xx**

Trace and write.

X X X X X

X X X X X

NAME _____

Trace and write.

X-ray

xylophone

exclamation

extinct

Lesson 1.20   The Letter **Zz**

Trace and write.

Z — Z — Z — Z — Z

z — z — z — z — z

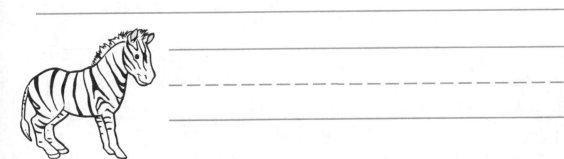

Lesson 1.20   The Letter **Zz**

Trace and write.

zigzag

zebra

zero

zoo

Lesson 1.21   The Letter **Mm**

Trace and write.

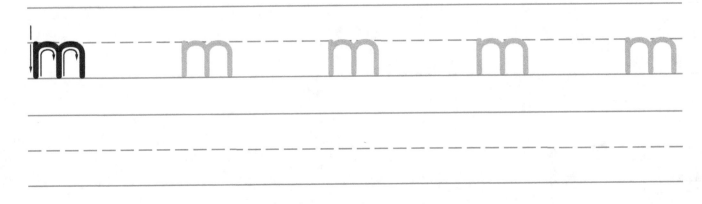

Lesson 1.21 The Letter **Mm**

Trace and write.

Madison

measure

misspell

meter

Lesson 1.22   The Letter **Nn**

Trace and write.

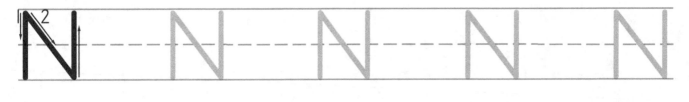

Lesson 1.22 The Letter **Nn**

Trace and write.

Nebraska

nickel

noun

nest

Lesson 1.23 The Letter **Rr**

Trace and write.

R R R R R

r r r r r

Spectrum Manuscript Handwriting
Grades K–2

Chapter 1 Lesson 23
Letters and Words

Lesson 1.23 The Letter **Rr**

Trace and write.

Rhode Island

resources

rectangle

rhyme

Lesson 1.24 The Letter **Hh**

Trace and write.

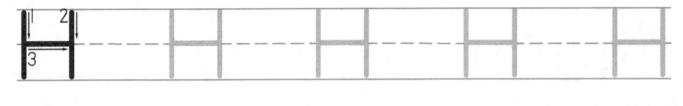

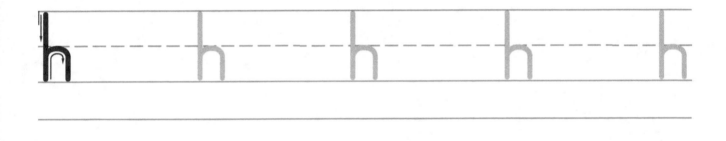

Chapter 1 Lesson 24
Letters and Words

Lesson 1.24 The Letter **Hh**

Trace and write.

Hawaii

homophone

height

heat

Lesson 1.25 The Letter **Bb**

Trace and write.

B   B   B   B   B

b   b   b   b   b

Lesson 1.25 The Letter **Bb**

Trace and write.

Boston
_____

beginning
_____

boiling
_____

bear
_____

Lesson 1.26 The Letter **Pp**

Trace and write.

P P P P P

p p p p p

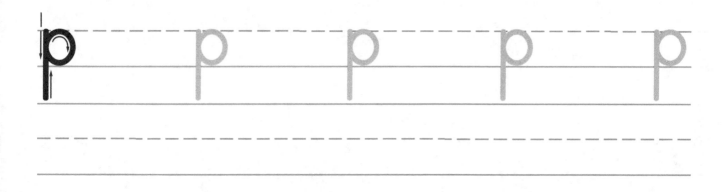

Lesson 1.26 The Letter **Pp**

Trace and write.

Phoenix

predicate

pentagon

present

Write the sentence.

Add Alaska to
the map.

Lesson 2.2   The Letter **Dd**

Write the sentence.

It's donut day for Dan.

Lesson 2.3   The Letter **Gg**

Write the sentence.

Gabe grows great grapes.

Review Lessons 2.1–2.3   The Letters **Aa**, **Dd**, and **Gg**

Review

Write the sentence.

Dad gave goats as a gag.

Lesson 2.4   The Letter **Qq**

Write the sentence.

Quebec
requested the
queen.

Lesson 2.5   The Letter **Cc**

Write the sentence.

Clouds covered Connecticut.

Lesson 2.6   The Letter **Ee**

Write the sentence.

Eight Englishmen
eat eel.

NAME _____

The Letters **Qq**, **Cc**, and **Ee**

Write the sentence.

Quentin quit
every club but
croquet.

Review

Lesson 2.7   The Letter **Oo**

Write the sentence.

Oklahoma has
no octopuses.

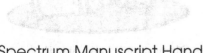

Lesson 2.8   The Letter **Uu**

Write the sentence.

Uncle Umbert

cut a rug.

Review Lessons 2.7–2.8   The Letters **Oo** and **Uu**

Review

Write the sentence.

How about the mouse at your house?

Review: Chapter 2 Lessons 7–8
Sentences

Lesson 2.9 The Letter **Ss**

Write the sentence.

The Sun is our
solar system's
star.

Lesson 2.10 The Letter **Ff**

Write the sentence.

The fifth fluffy
ferret is Felicia's.

Review Lessons 2.9–2.10 The Letters **Ss** and **Ff**

Write the sentence.

Did Fred find Sam's socks in the safe?

Lesson 2.11 The Letter **Ll**

Write the sentence.

Lily's llama lives
on level land.

Lesson 2.12 The Letter Ii

Write the sentence.

Isabel inched
into the igloo.

NAME _____

Write the sentence.

The temperature is ten degrees too hot.

Lesson 2.14 The Letter **Jj**

Write the sentence.

Judge Jones
jumped for joy.

NAME _____

Write the sentence.

Jin just lost his letter to Lincoln.

Lesson 2.15 The Letter **Kk**

Write the sentence.

Kris kept her
kite in Kansas.

Lesson 2.16 The Letter **Yy**

Write the sentence.

Yes, you may yap
at your yak.

Lesson 2.17 The Letter **Vv**

Write the sentence.

Victor viewed a
video on verbs.

NAME _____

Write the sentence.

Violet's very yellow van makes the trek!

Lesson 2.18 The Letter **Ww**

Write the sentence.

Wanda wears
water wings.

Lesson 2.19   The Letter **Xx**

Write the sentence.

Xiang explained
that foxes are
not extinct.

Lesson 2.20 The Letter **Zz**

Write the sentence.

The bee
zigzagged to
Zelda's Zoo.

Review Lessons 2.18–2.20 The Letters **Ww**, **Xx**, and **Zz**

Write the sentence.

Xavier's wizard
is a whiz at
xylophone!

Lesson 2.21 The Letter **Mm**

Write the sentence.

My mom misspelled my name!

Lesson 2.22 The Letter **Nn**

Write the sentence.

Names of towns

are nouns.

Lesson 2.23   The Letter **Rr**

Write the sentence.

Ryan is trying
to rhyme on time.

Review

Write the sentence.

Ramona's red
macaw named
Nannette is near.

NAME _____

Write the sentence.

Please heat up Hannah's hotdog.

Lesson 2.25   The Letter **Bb**

Write the sentence.

Bindi buys Boston
baked beans.

Lesson 2.26 The Letter **Pp**

Write the sentence.

Purple pentagons
popped up.

Write the sentence.

Proud parents hug a happy baby bat.

Final Review **A-Z** Sentences

The sentence below uses all letters of the alphabet. Use it to practice
your handwriting.

The wizard's very big ox jumped quickly for change.

A-Z Sentences

The sentence below uses all letters of the alphabet. Use it to practice your handwriting.

A dozen brave ex-knights will quest for juicy plums.